« THE GLORIOUS FLIGHT »

Alice and Martin Provensen

THE
GLORIOUS
FLIGHT

ACROSS
THE CHANNEL
WITH LOUIS BLÉRIOT
JULY 25, 1909

PUFFIN BOOKS   NEW YORK

It all began one morning.

Mr. Louis Blériot, his oldest daughter Alceste,
his daughter of four years Charmaine,
his third daughter Suzette,
his son Jeannot,
their mama Alice, and the baby Gabrielle,
also the cat Minou,
their little dog Arsène,
and the big cockatoo Chloë
have just had their breakfast.

The year is 1901.
The place is the city of Cambrai, in France.

It is a beautiful day. The sun is shining. Papa Blériot and all his family

(except Minou the cat and Chloë the cockatoo) are going for a ride in their shiny new car.

As they roll up the street, they hear, far above in the sky, a strange sound.
Clacketa...clacketa...clacketa...
"Hark!" says Papa Blériot. He does not look where he is going.

Just ahead, on the narrow street, is the wagon of Alphonse Juvet,
full of pumpkins.
Also his son César, and many cabbages.

"*CRUMP!*" goes the car. Into the cart of Alphonse Juvet.
The strange sound from the air is forgotten.
Papa Blériot was driving very slowly, but even so the cart is on its side.

Pumpkins all over!

No one is hurt, but there are bruised cabbages and angry faces.

Fists are raised. The policeman, Achille Duval, poises his pencil, when...

Clacketa, Clacketa. CLACKETA! CLACKETA!

Out of the clouds, right over their heads, soars a great white airship.

And a man is sitting in a basket, driving it through the air!

What a wonderful sight! It is the first airship seen over the city of Cambrai.
Papa Blériot invites everyone to the café. They toast the valiant aeronaut and each other.
And César, the brave Juvet boy. And the pumpkins. Everyone is happy.

13

Everyone but Louis Blériot.
Now he has only one wish.
He says to his family,
"I, too, will build a flying machine,
A great white bird.
We will work hard.
We will all fly through the air like swallows!"

So here is «BLÉRIOT I.»
No one is small enough to sit in it but Minou.
And she will not.
It has a little motor to make the wings flap.
Alas! It flaps like a chicken.
Never mind.

This is more like it. Here is «BLÉRIOT II,» a glider. Big enough to hold a man.
Papa has not yet learned to pilot, so Gabriel Voisin, his good friend, will fly.

A motorboat will tow it into the air as the glider has no motor.
All is in readiness. Gabriel gives the signal.

Away roars the motorboat.
Like a great swan, the beautiful glider rises into the air…

…and shoots down into the river with a splash that frightens the fishes.
Gabriel Voisin is wet but not hurt. "We almost flew!" he says.

Papa has decided to learn to fly himself.

«BLÉRIOT III» has a fine motor and propeller, but it will not take off from the water.

So Papa gives it two motors and two propellers to make «Blériot IV.»
«Blériot IV» goes in beautiful circles. Papa is learning.

«BLÉRIOT V» hops over the ground like a rabbit.
Papa is getting lots of practice.

But «Blériot VI»!
It sails across a whole field before it hits a rock. Not so bad!

And with «Blériot VII»
Papa has an aeroplane
that really can fly.

No matter that the inevitable happens.
A slight crash...
a broken rib,
a black eye
to add to the list of
breaks, sprains, and bruises
over the past six years.

Now Papa is a real flier.
And the «BLÉRIOT» is a real aeroplane.
How proud Alceste, Charmaine, Suzette
Jeannot, Gabrielle, and Mama are!

Only one thing remains.
To prove how good the aeroplane is.
To show the world what it can do.
As if to light the spark,
a great prize is offered to the first man
to fly across the English Channel.

Twenty miles wide.
Black, tossing waves.
Fog and rain.
A very cold bath.
A long swim.
It is a dangerous prospect.
Just what Papa likes.

For Perseverance and Valor
£1,000.
—POUNDS STERLING—
OFFERED BY LORD NORTHCLIFF
Proprietor of The

London Daily Mail
TO
THE FIRST MAN
TO FLY THE CHANNEL

FRANCE ENGLAND

COAST TO COAST
In Either Direction
Between Sunrise and Sunset
without intermediate landings

£1000.
PRIZE
For Information & Applications
INTERESTED PARTIES SHOULD
INQUIRE AT OFFICE

On July 25, 1909, as the sun rises, Papa Blériot walks with his crutch
(a minor flying accident, nothing serious)
out to the field where his plane, «Blériot xi,» waits.

He kisses Alceste, Charmaine, Suzette, Jeannot, Gabrielle, and Mama Blériot.
Papa climbs into the cockpit. His friend Alfred Le Blanc spins the propeller.
It is 4:35 a.m.

The motor coughs. Sputters. Roars. Down the grassy field «Blériot XI» bumps.

She picks up speed and suddenly climbs into the sky.

The French coast disappears.
Far below is the destroyer *Escopette*,
waiting to pick up Papa if his motor fails…
if they can find him in time.

Ten minutes tick by.
The waves reach up to catch the tiny plane.

Now there is nothing but swirling fog.
No France, no England, no waves.
Papa is alone.
Lost.

He sits motionless,
not touching the steering lever,
and lets the plane go where it will.

Suddenly…

The white cliffs of Dover flash beneath him. A wonderful moment!

Thirty-six minutes after taking off from France, Papa is over England.

Papa stops his engine and makes a very bad landing. As usual!
Never mind about a broken propeller. Louis Blériot is in England!

He flew there in thirty-seven minutes. What a shout goes up!
Truly, it was a glorious flight.

Louis Blériot (1872-1936) was one of the truly great pioneers of aviation.
He devoted the fortune acquired by his invention of an automobile searchlight
to the development and construction of his high-performance aircraft,
the «BLÉRIOT XI.» His flight across the English Channel demonstrated to the
world that barriers of land and sea no longer existed for the airplane.

PUFFIN BOOKS
Published by the Penguin Group
Penguin Putnam Books for Young Readers, 345 Hudson Street, New York, New York 10014, U.S.A.
Penguin Books Ltd, 27 Wrights Lane, London W8 5TZ, England
Penguin Books Australia Ltd, Ringwood, Victoria, Australia
Penguin Books Canada Ltd, 10 Alcorn Avenue, Toronto, Ontario, Canada M4V 3B2
Penguin Books (N.Z.) Ltd, 182-190 Wairau Road, Auckland 10, New Zealand

Penguin Books Ltd, Registered Offices: Harmondsworth, Middlesex, England

First published by Viking Penguin Inc. 1983
Published in Picture Puffins 1987

48 49 50

We would like to acknowledge, with gratitude, the help given us in researching
The Glorious Flight by Catherine Deloraine and Richard King.   A. & M. P.

Library of Congress Cataloging in Publication Data
Provensen, Alice.   The glorious flight.
Reprint. Originally published: New York: The Viking Press, 1983.
Summary: A biography of the man whose fascination with flying machines produced the Blériot XI,
which in 1909 became the first heavier-than-air
machine to fly the English Channel.
1. Blériot, Louis, 1872–1936—Juvenile literature.   [1. Blériot, Louis, 1872–1936.   2. Air pilots.
3. Airplanes—Design and construction]   I. Provensen, Martin.
II. Title. TL721.B5P76   1987
629.13′092′4   [B]   [92]   86-25473   ISBN 978-0-140-50729-4